Strange Terrain

Matthew James Babcock

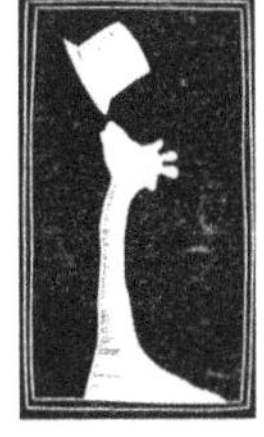

MadHat Press
Asheville, North Carolina

MadHat Press
MadHat Incorporated
PO Box 8364, Asheville, NC 28814

The Library of Congress has assigned
this edition a Control Number of
2016914693

ISBN 978-1-941196-36-6 (paperback)

Cover art and design by Marc Vincenz
Book design by MadHat Press

www.MadHat-Press.com

First Printing

Table of Contents

I. THE PRISON OF THE AIR

II. LOOSE MOON

III. HEART AND ROOT

IV. SPARE CHANGES

Even in ordinary moonlight, what building,
what tree, what passer on the otherwise unlighted road
is not steeped in strangeness?

—Robert Francis

I was the world in which I walked, and what I saw
Or heard or felt came not but from myself:
And there I found myself more truly and more strange

—Wallace Stevens

to my clan
for loving this strange man

I

The Prison of the Air

Idaho Étude: I

Mule deer tracks
  pound unbound cadences
    of azure absence
as soundless as
  the white blaze
    of faultless snowfall
March third above
  the road to
    Victor. All warmth
scrounges husks of
  sun. Eleven rivers
    crush cattail quills
in ragged icework,
  scrawl serrated silences
    throughout cutthroat trout
hover and drone.
  Switchback ferret shuttles
    erratic blue sluice
of aspen shadow
  across winter monochrome.
    Motion echoes eclipse.
Summer hunger throbs
  in blood of
    dusk, rusts venom
pulse of berries,
  stings branch tips
    with shriveled slings.
Thaws plummet through
  the wavering ground.
    The clash and

scrape of moonlight
escapes the space
that it surrounds.

Idaho Étude: 2

Then sandhill crane,
reconnaissance of sky.
Then Stock Building

supply, 2X4 payload.
Then gradual ghost,
beaver riverbend trove.

Then vacant alley,
staccato ice ruts.
Then osprey acrobat

impales Robinson Creek.
Then Bob's Texaco
appreciates your business.

Then lava rock lichen,
architecture of yellow.
Then roadside beer can,

prelude to gleam.
Then mastodon mud,
coda of scapula.

Then ditchbank rope swing,
milkweed doxology.
Then ochre daybreak

invokes antelope caravan.
Then sheep skull
socket, continent crescendo.

Then aquifer torrent
howls turbulent blue.
Then savage glacier,

fissure of sun.
Then barbed outcropping,
finger and thumb.

Idaho Étude: 3

butte
about
abut
beauty
drought
burned
brought
about
bright
brittle
breach
rich
rout
root
rot
rut
riot
reach
ranch
brand
bland
bleach
branch
brought
broad
route
about
butte

Idaho Étude: 4

Sequence woodsmoke starlings. Camouflage screech owl
cameo. Radiate brushfire iris. Moulder backhoe
monument. Careen triple railroad crossing.
Collide meteorite crater. Scorch ghost
town: Squirrel. Parallel paradise
parallax. Escape sagebrush
escutcheon. Muse magpie
mosaic. Bombard junk B-29.
Waver county airport
weeds. Free pool Sunday
tavern. Chromatic
pheasant cattle guard.
Tread artifact tractor.
Barrage barbed wire
burrs. Seagull
landfill stench.
Time dry
riverbed
trench.

IDAHO ÉTUDE: 5

Aprillianthilluminealderangeodesideratariidstrata

corefugenesiskindlevelingerosionaturanaturata

sunslantangleachwranglerdriveinnumerablebbandarch

buzzsawindependentedpickupsurgenterrainstainedMarch

The Way My Three-Year Old Daughter Runs Naked through the House Early Wednesday Evening

The way my three-year old daughter
runs naked through the house
early Wednesday evening in October
confirms my belief that the soul

is a little girl always
breaking from her father's grip
in the parking lot of Family Dollar
to harass box elder bugs,

or toppling jigsaw puzzles from card tables
at garage sales where the blissful air
ripens the lemon-lime twist
of Hispanic syllables and cloud-headed

retired couples unload cankered golf shoes
and framed Swiss prints before
moving to beachfront suites in New Zealand.
The way I stare out the window

after chasing her to bed reveals
that the spirit is the last robin
of the season, its vestments
stabbed the dusky bloodstain

of shortening days, its arresting plea
as a common breed to stay erect

and set fast a noiseless grip
before fleeing such uncommon poise.

The way October labels all sales final
and, unsentimental, dumps its remaining
trinkets in a battered shoebox
before boarding up a vacant home

from whose sagging rafters
nuthatches scatter through
unpatched cobweb hammocks
reminds me of the speed of the day

when the small nude girl of the self
will tear free and scamper out
a screen door blown open by the breeze,
shooing away brindled cats and drawing smiles

from bemused neighbors who,
dreaming they stroll barefoot
on vanilla beaches in insurance calendar photos,
comb fingers through the picked-over

remains of Holstein cow oven mitts,
canary neckties, and potpourri jars
in which someone has tossed with
marbles and packets of dried pumpkin seeds

my last unanswered need, the unfinished
puzzle of what my last words decreed.

Matthew James Babcock

Miniature Golf Karma

Surely the dollar I stash
in the Kerr jar marked
"College Fund" on the ice cream
counter at Mr. Pudder's
outside Sennett, New York,

will persuade the gods of July
to preserve my daughters
from famine and disease.
The five bucks I stuff
through the coleslaw bucket lid

outside Quality Markets in Erie
means McDowell's Girls Basketball
will skyhook my fortune
through the frayed net
of the cosmos to beat the buzzer.

Daily fate challenges our spot
in the Quad Cities Tourney.
Nature knocks the inner man
through the mouse hole doorway
in the mechanized windmill, rebounds off

milk cans and skids up Astroturf ramps
into the clown's plywood yawn
for free games. As surely as
the giver begs at the entrance,
the bulldog grandmother who peddles

produce in the parking lot
of Church's Chicken in Independence,
shameless of her summer squash
arms and legs, knows when
I don't buy tomatoes as bright

as the blood of August,
I trade legacies with
the destroying angel who
scrawls death sentences in graffiti
on the train trestle past

Bell Township, Pennsylvania, from
whose struts and concrete parapets
paunchy teenage girls
in obscenely skimpy bikinis
plunge into the copper oblivion

of the river, while overhead
screaming red-tailed hawks churn
the atmosphere in a daredevil ballet
in which the victor rakes talons
through the vanquished blue fish of sky.

Matthew James Babcock

Kissing Booth: Twenty-Seven Years Later

When I reveal my weight to Kim Edelmeyer
(née Schlund), the nurse at Community Care
on Memorial Day, I wonder if she remembers.
Her pen dots a smile on her clipboard.
The light of a thousand ordinary afternoons
wets her eyes. The monitor she clips
on my fingertip draws from me the news
that my parents are fine in Prescott Valley.
I report no allergies, and she chronicles
the new stretch on the Bob Barton Highway
that her folks said shaved thousands off
their home value. What of Big Brett, her brother
who boxed the Gooding rowdies in
the Smoker Benefits? Old friends? Jocks?
Dweebs? Our conversation treats
returning home like a pox we've
dodged for decades. Nothing cures
the unspoken. History is its own dose.
From the box theater of the otoscope
she slips in my ear, we peer into the past.
Ponytailed, she sits with Christy Davidson
in the high school cafeteria for the senior choir
fundraiser. My ninth grade friends wave
a dollar and prescribe a dare. Air hisses
into the cuff squeezing my bicep.
Her hands guide my head to her face,
and she kisses me in front of the waiting world.
My blood rises to the level of love.

She steps back, examines me. The years
swing her body into a bag of unwashed scrubs.
Her face slackens, a sack of mother's masks,
and all this time, I have been immune to sorrow.

Matthew James Babcock

Lima

Believe, if you can, you are stopping
in Peru and not Montana. Believe,
as you gas up at Ralph's Exxon & Convenience
under a sky of hallucinogenic blue,
your parents and children (who are
traveling with you) are not gimpy orphans
vending Chiclets or thugs poised
to swipe razor blades through purse straps
on the arms of women in the Crazy Critters
Bingo League. Look around. Envision
North in South America: adobe hills,
wind carding yellow grass, clouds as white
as the January that Pizarro's churches
scrubbed the Rímac Valley of every Incan oracle
to pave a City of Kings. Holster the nozzle
in the pump, and in the rain-scarred
rearview mirror see yourself as parent and child.
Be transported. Follow your generations
inside to pay and count the buildings
that mimic *pueblos jóvenes*. A pink hotel
called The Peat that commands, "Cook
Your Own Steak!" Jan's Café crying
"Welcome Hunters!" and "Home-cooked Grub!"
Under a stuffed coyote priced at
five hundred dollars, listen to your father
tell the cashier how in 1961, when he
was a bellhop in Wyoming, he checked
Ansel Adams into Jenny Lake Lodge. Spy no
shish-kebabbed deep-fried guinea pigs
in the stainless-steel food warmers. Sigh

and buy your three daughters eight-packs
of B'loonies made by a company in Jacksonville.
In the car, strap on the seatbelt of what
history has revealed. Ascend the onramp
of knowing that of all the world's scams,
the most footloose is that you must travel one way.
Count the others: 1) believe; 2) remember;
3) save space for turning tourist
in the conquest of the present hour, a figure
wandering into the black and white landscape
of forgetfulness, where you pause
with folk parcels of powdered aphrodisiacs
and anti-depressants to watch a woman
with a toothless smile unravel the scarlet thread
of your pulse from an alpaca blanket
in the photo you think twice about taking.

Matthew James Babcock

Jerusalem Artichoke

after visiting the Religious Reflection Room in the Detroit Metro Airport

In The Squatter's Pub Brewery, two pilots
 (I hope not mine) quaff beer
and devour Black and Bleu Rocket Wraps.
 The label on the Odwalla's bottle
from which I sip green puree says I have
 swallowed Jerusalem artichoke,
a plant that, contrary to what its name
 might suggest, is not an artichoke
and not from Jerusalem. This is
 the equation of life: Nothing is what
it says it is. Despite the high price,
 somehow this is healthy. The Italian,
girasole, means "sunflower."
 After Samuel de Champlain dispatched
shiploads of the bundled tubers
 from Cape Cod to France, people
added "sunroot" and "earth apple"
 to the legend. What is prayer but
a commerce of discoveries? When
 is misunderstanding a pilgrimage?
Some days, the greatest risk
 can be to sit and stare
at the intoxicating flight of daylight
 through two glasses of amber.
This is, after all, the quest of the new world.
 To drink the strange. To explore
without leaving. To grow into the myth
 of your name and, having exiled
the nomad eye, make a holy city of the heart.

Saturday Bike Ride (Unity of the Self)

Blame the gray metaphysics of the last
  pure weekend in November
if I jettison the exoskeleton of parenthood
  and pedal on stainless-steel breezes
back through time to the vacant lot
  across from my house on Davis Street.
Ask The Illuminati how I inhale
  my present age then exhale three decades.

Even Hegel's *Geist* couldn't explain how
  I carom on bad gears over railroad tracks,
past the Steiner silos, and on the far side
  astral project astride a purple Western Auto
Buzz Bike banana seat with sissy bar,
  transported in copper Toughskin jeans
to Darbi Neff's driveway, the Lone Ranger
  in J. C. Penney's shoebox under my arm.

My *doppelgänger* shuttles by the fairgrounds
  home arts building: an old man in a Kiwanis
jacket, piloting a three-wheeler in whose
  chrome basket my kid fears shine
like aluminum cans. At the airport, a flicker
  screech drags across the scuffed board
of sky, recycles in mid-air the hollow tree
  where Jeff Dehlin hid Camels and *Playboy*.

Keep your caskets. Dig my grave in Hanley Morris's
  back yard with an army surplus shovel
from Koppel's Browzeville. In underground fort,

stockpile Brach's Medley and saltines.
Track the erratic philosophies of nighthawks
in sky as black as the ace of spades
clothespinned to strike spokes. Let the throttle's
holy racket spur you into the next hill.

Junior Gymnastics Karma

On the overcast winter afternoon
you dub yourself Cynic of the Age
travel with my daughter and me
to the Crystal Cup at Salt Lake Community College
and watch her and three hundred
prepubescent pixies torch history's tournament
of blood with their smiles. Do not doubt.
The sports complex of the cosmos
turns on the sacred torque of give and take.
Thus saith the sturdy woman in
Mighty Mites Cheer and Dance jacket
who provides laser-green wristbands
at the entrance. She pronounces blessings
on you when you pay instead of sneak
in the back. Her life's wages: a door-knob
nose, a figure like a sack of produce.
Her grin of broken teeth gleams
like a rain gutter shaggy with January ice.
This world is judgment. Final scores
sift sequins on snow. Long drives
end in long waits. Chump-change scholarships
chain gorgeous Lithuanian women
to the Saturday shift in the snack bar,
the lanky beauty of their volleyball
uniforms the only fair exchange
for three-dollar hot dogs and popcorn.
And you—head bowed on the stand,
awaiting the executioner's medal, its surface
embossed with bazookas spouting
bouquets of flame, corpses backbending in

mass graves, helicopters applauding
for starving orphans. If you strap on the sexless
leotard of your soul and assemble
at the gate with the spangled ranks from
Top Flight, Idaho Elite, Tiny Titans,
and the team in shimmery peach who flew in
from Texas and swept the all-around—
if you don't commit the unpardonable sin
of blinding yourself for spite, you might
arc through the lights and land forever
on the morning someone drove
all day to award you the ceremony of your birth.

Reunion

At MacGregor's Grill & Tap Room I become one
with my true self the moment Tom McCusker—
single, schnockered, father of a little boy—shoulders
from the sweaty grottos of Herman Melville's dreams
through the Penfield High School Class of '91
to see if he still might have a chance with my wife
after twenty years. Platters of cherry tomatoes
and asparagus spears lie untouched on shellacked
pine tables. Beer mugs swing fistfuls of Spanish gold
over the trophy for Best Homecoming Float
and the glittery shrine for Eric (gunned down
in a drug deal) and Towanda (found on railroad tracks
six days after the ten-year). The conversation in the room
sounds like a passenger jet doing an engine test.
So when Tom McCusker, in skin-tight black T-shirt
and diamond crucifix, extends his hand, I hear only
what my wife said the week before our trip to New York:
Tom was from Glasgow and days before our flight
sent her a note, asking if she would have liked him
if she hadn't liked her boyfriend, Chris. I have journeyed
thousands of miles to crush Tom's grip and say,
We aren't in high school anymore. People stopped leaving
the British Empire to seek fortune in the New World hundreds
of years ago. Instead, the history of conquest pulses
through our handclasp. The waitress transforms us
from rivals to twins separated at birth by shipwreck.
Out the window, Irondequoit Bay brews the red ale
of dusk. I want to tell Tom I remember when love
was a leaky sloop soldiering out of the Firth of Forth
and arriving every day in the same malarial swamp

of lies and loneliness. I came to stand under the thump
of the house PA and say, *Tom McCusker, you are*
the MC Hammer tunes nobody hears. Your life is the U.S.-Australia
softball game no one watches on the big screen TV. But I leave,
swearing to my long-lost blood brother I will give him
the deed to my sugar plantation, with my wife
and five children as slaves, and sail the globe to find
the marooned mutineer I no longer recognize as myself.

Statistics from My Daughter's Sixth-Grade Choir Concert

When Miss Hale, one third through her reproductive years,
herds her class onto the risers for Greg Gilpin's
"Do You Feel the Rhythm?" we clap. Not as
hermaphrodites announcing our presence in rural India,
but as proud parents of kids in black and aquamarine
Choir is Epic! T-shirts. My girl shifts from foot to foot,
and I count twenty students over to find a boy
with an extra rib. The Down's Syndrome redhead
in blueberry sneakers—Miss Hale's future son, the longer
she waits to have children—grins and releases nearly all
of the 1.5 pints of gas he produces daily. Between
Curry's "Down to the River to Pray" and Albrecht's
"Won't Grow Up," I'm transformed. I become
a Gallup lightning rod for fifty-seven percent
of people in Cleveland's City Hall on National Prayer
Day and skyrocketing dwarfism rates. From the back,
a cough, at sixty miles per hour, punctures an
awkward pause as the pianist's fingernails grow
faster than her toenails. Who are these youngsters?
I wonder as they get down-and-dirty-go-go-dancer
for McFerrin's "Don't Worry, Be Happy." Will they
be allergic to deodorant and milk? Who will tell them
they have brains faster than computers, bones stronger
than steel? Which one of ten finger-popping cuties
will send a nude photo of herself to a crush then twine
a scarf in a treble clef around her neck the night
her mother screams an aria in a house filling up with
two pounds of shed skin per person? Bang. Bang.

Miss Hale's fairy baton drops them like shooting gallery
ducks into cancer, fallen arches, and waterborne waste.
Then my girl looks at me. And I know she will use
all 600,000 of her breaths to adopt black dogs. Already,
her taste buds outnumber mine. Her heartbeat sprints
ahead of the stony riverbeds five pints of blood paint
through my veins. Already, her glance rewrites the world's
songbook of facts, the epic slogan on the T-shirt
that says we will lick our elbows. We will love longer
than chewing gum stays in the stomach. We will
sing when we have to let go of our 75 to 100 trillion cells.

Nostalgia for Teenagers

Those were storybook days. I rode
a sleepy tide of translucent pink.
I roved as red nucleus, mute supernova,
cosmonaut of The Black Nowhere,
psychopomp of saline dreams. Talking
of the past summons language
impossible to you in your youth.
Nothing compares to the jeweled cages
of veins through which my thoughts
knifed like brilliant bluebirds. Who bolted
the sonic windows? When did hunger
skim the webbing from between
my toes? I would give anything for
sadness to sugarcoat my tongue
at the sound of secrets from strangers,
for the shouts of neighbors to seep
through the stained-glass membranes
like whale songs played on French horns.
If only I could somersault again
in the elliptical echo of my uncle's
melancholy laugh, press my face
against the purr of playgrounds. I miss
paradoxes the most. Long mornings
of midnight. The slippery walls of my cell.
My navel a rubber band ready to unravel
and lasso Saturn. If I could just go back—
then when I rise, as I do every day
to roam this corridor of perpetual dusk,
I would see each trip as a passage
I've already made. This time, I wouldn't wait

to float barefoot in my jumpsuit of mercury
toward the illuminated door. I would
relish not knowing if anything came before.

The Spring Olympics

There would be one event: The Bloom.
To train, make all living things your team.
Lean your head ten times a day against
the same cold window, breathing steam.
Watch coliseums of snow melt gritty maps
of March into the parking lot behind
Mountain Ridge Apartments. The blind man
coaching his seeing-eye dog can shave
seconds off your memory. Recall when
you were six: running lit a torch in your lungs.
Eleven: biking to school, you broke
the record for youthful hope. Twenty-eight:
the losing streak of the present moved
the tape to thirty-seven, when years
became sprints. To never forget
the glory, parade with the ambassadors
of May. Let your eyes track the archery
of gnats. Follow the tae kwon do of tulips
as the sunset blasts clay pigeons
of white glare over a stadium of rowdy peaks.
Cheer for the young lovers who lug
backpacks and argue out of earshot
on your street. They pivot, hold each other
like skaters setting for a lift, his skin
as pale as the Athenian sun that outlasted
Pheidippides, her hair as black as the streak
Jesse Owens ran through Hitler's blindness.
Score his attempts to kiss her. Her downward
gaze concedes nothing but her cheek,
then a silent starter's pistol sends them off,

holding hands, at staggered paces,
unsure if they should drop the baton
keeping them breathless in this race with no end.

Passage

When I hear that over the last three months
in the patchwork jungles of the Oriente
a Secoya shaman named Cesario
staged an elaborate ritual celebrating

his young son's foray into manhood, all I can
think is that nothing
like that
ever happened for me.

Now it seems the quintessential tragedy—
that I have no remembered rite
to mull over, no anklet
string of hermit crab shells or quincunx

of pulsing torches that signified the moment,
my teenage palate baptized
by the dregs of a bitter hallucinogenic tea
made from pureed bamboo or black mangrove,

the thunderhead tiers and red skyline
west of Quito an erotic dream.
Perhaps in my case there was nothing more
to mark the event than a shifting

of body cells, like the collapse
of an old staircase in an abandoned
house, a slumped coil of DNA
the hundredth time I walked past

the Reverend Tommy Carlson's blue house
with my incomplete social studies homework,
or a mute fanfare of nothing hallooed
from a small conch shell in my ear

as I sat staring out my bedroom window
at the calligraphy of the wind
on the alfalfa fields,
an empty green Mead notebook in my hands

for a diary. Perhaps my Ecuadorean bar mitzvah
came while I was mowing the lawn
on a Saturday, mourning the loss
of Sam, the family cat,

or something not so epic—I yawned
while pumping gas into
my mom's convertible Volkswagen Rabbit
at a Texaco outside American Falls

and made the change, from chrysalis
to the whisper of a red admiral,
streaking thumb smudges of vermilion paint
over my eyebrows as I replaced the nozzle,

catching a whiff of woodsmoke incense off
Seagull Bay and a few stray phonemes
from the chanted mantra of a passing semi truck.
Maybe that's how it happened.

That day, the Galapagos Fur Seal still launched
acrobatic loop-de-loops beneath
the symphonic crash of the waves,
in sync with the streamlined centuries

of endemic breeding cycles.
And the Waved Albatross didn't regard
my monumental shift in the slightest
but instead succumbed to another bizarre series

of rapturous fits, gooney bird fencing matches
spurred on by paroxysms of love and hope.
Around the planet things
rolled on as if it were 1835 all over again

and Darwin, scribbling nothing of my evolution
in the margins of his notes, packed up shop
and headed back to *The Beagle*,
giddy but exhausted,

feeling like a kid again, in his
head a purple menagerie of fourteen new finches.

Matthew James Babcock

Even Now

Even now the timber wolf that loped
   in slippers of thunder through
      spring drizzle north of Obsidian Creek
stalks the interlude of azure daylight
   in which I stop on the street to watch
      seven dancers rehearse in the old building
on College Avenue between Kenny and Larry's
   Barber Shop and Sammy's Café. Under charcoal clouds,
      we pulled off the road and with binoculars
tracked its nimble trot into the yellow of willows.
   Claws of copper lightning raked its gunsmoke fur.
      An assassin's grace drove its soundless gait,
its coat as dense as myth. It vanished the way these
   dancers sway then leap from the parquet
      floorboards of Thursday into the glacial mirrors
of themselves. Even now thugs who beat
   a man to death at two a.m. outside my room
      at the Westminster Hotel haunt the backstreets
of Bayswater. Unseen, they chassé for a cigarette
   and *Daily Mirror*, shiftless at bus stops
      in the grubby leotards of their skins. The bark
of the man who paid them—*Fook 'im up, lads!*
   Fook 'im up, lads!—shakes the shaggy hedges
      around Leinster Square. The shimmering red pool
the street sweeper missed on the sidewalk
   the next morning rises to become weather.
      The world's roots feed on blood of rain.
For every novice hitman, there is a small-town
   ballerina. In the refurbished studio of the soul,
      intervals of blue illumine flaked whitewash

and borrowed chairs. April tosses its swan partner
  to the evergreen rafters and catches in October jaws
    the broken costume of a snowshoe hare.
Even the earth's most savage pirouettes end
  in stunning feats of balance, a rhythm
    and hunger that beats time on a battered surface
that was uneven then but is even now.

Matthew James Babcock

Threnody for an Idaho Spring

The unexpected thaw musters inmates
to the sidewalk outside Arrowhead Mortgage.
Fresh from the Narrenturm, they scrape
gray slush from concrete with scoop
shovels and train electroshock gazes
on the traffic of the free world.
The surging temperature gives them leave
to labor in loose orange and white
candystripe sleeves. Good-old-boy
trios chaperone in navy blue, badges
glinting like stolen sun. Everywhere,
mere movement grants asylum.
Frosted hatchbacks hobble through
the pharmacy's nickelodeon, craving
opiates of exhaust and newspaper.
Gutter floods babble muddy bedlam.
The ranch outfitter's marquee boasts
the cheapest Annie Oakley perfume.
Only birds are delivered. Starling
chain gangs break from slack telephone
wires above the roof of Thomas Vacuum
Sales & Service. Through the notch
in a crow's wing, February flashes
the unfinished history of the madhouse
of the sky. A downy woodpecker shrieks
an alarm, flees the shuddering spiral staircase
of an aspen sapling, its brilliant skull
patch the smudge of dawn blood
into which it vanishes. The rosy bark
of lindens glows in the blue cold

like slapped cheeks. On ordinary pilgrimage,
the unshaven citizen passes and tries
not to stare. Each step extends a corridor
of light that escapes the prison of the air.

Matthew James Babcock

Five Laotians

Eight days of winter storm warnings from Kalispell
to Soda Springs bring the five Laotians back
to my fourth-grade class at Central Elementary.
After lunch, they invaded state history, ushered in
by a school board official wearing a Popeye tie.
Eyes earthward, they glided to empty desks
like U.S. soldiers shuffling bloody boots through
opium fog. On the playground, we retreated.
From tetherball pole to bike rack, we tiptoed
a street-market savoir-faire through rice paddies
of unexploded cluster bombs. They huddled
around oil drum trash barrels like ousted diplomats.
Sibilant blizzards of spiced syllables dropped
barbecued beetles from their lips into banana leaf
baskets and *Peanuts* lunch buckets. We knew
nothing of Pathet Lao. In our nonage, 1975
was a golden age of math and basketball. In secret,
we relished their names: Phousavanh, over six feet tall
with Oscar Wilde hair; Chantavy, our favorite,
with tarantula-fuzz mustache; Phitsemay, whose
dazzling soccer skills didn't stop us from calling him
Pizza Hut. On St. Patrick's Day, these three
crossed the softball diamond on embassage
in the striped green tube socks we had advised them
to wear. *Suh-noh*, they said, pointing to white skiffs
glazing the grass around third base. Their grins
flashed necklaces of rare bones and seashells.
No, I corrected them. *Frost. Fuh-rost*, they echoed,
crestfallen. I didn't tell them that Pingkham,
the girl who spoke English like an Oxfordian,

had called me to say that Lili, the girl who
never smiled, wanted to sleep with me. I didn't show
them Lili's passport photo on the Gano-Dehlin Insurance
keychain in my pocket. Later, I would laugh
at the image Pingkham's claim colored in my mind:
Lili and I in pajamas and sleeping bags, eating
potato chips and watching cartoons. Later, I would
learn life is more than sex and semantics. I would awake
in the school of my most exotic Januaries to see
my remaining days as the slow strain of water
through green tea leaves. All remaining light, the sun
riding one million elephants over hills of strange terrain.

II

Loose Moon

MITTELSCHMERZ

It's simple: On the same Saturday morning an eighty-six-year-old woman named Vera she has visited for seven years dies, she reports the sudden charge of a rampaging tide as red as banners. Days before, she read how the central ache swerving her off her axis into dizzy black space was due to the small translucent sphere that would have been our child anchoring itself like a stalled rock climber to her inner wall. I listened to her with all the rapt attention of a tenderfoot scout pretending not to hear a ghost story or an urban commuter on a street corner in his city's womb of sunlit smog caught hoping a suicidal businessman might jump from a suspension bridge. It's as simple as knowing death is the birth of our stories. She says Vera said after outliving two cheating and lying husbands who abandoned her, she couldn't wait to see her brother who died young from a punctured testicle and who stood up to the mother who beat her because Vera had been the unwanted pregnancy that had forced the marriage. It isn't that simple: the crippled wings of relief that lift me this morning at the kitchen window where I watch breakaway starlings rise from slack telephone lines like a broken blues chord above the earth whose core of hot blood ages the pain from which we fly by attaching ourselves to another.

Matthew James Babcock

Moose Remembered

This was when we were renting a house on the west side of town next to the Clean Spot
Laundromat and the red brick house owned by the mechanic with the ratty goatee
and AC/DC T-shirt who used to raise hell on Saturday mornings and send his wife
and small blond son running out the front door like refugees to find a cop cruiser
already parked at the curb. This was when I was compensating full-time for the little
I could give you and our baby girl, so early one Saturday morning while you slept
I trapped her in a blanket and carried her out on the driveway to watch a yearling
moose that had wandered into town from the Teton Basin. Its hide was the tacky
brown of an old leather sofa. With a connoisseur's fastidiousness, it nibbled leaves
from the lilac hedge barricades around La Jolla Apartments. This was when the usual
cop car arrived and, after a pause, started shooing the young moose down the road
with searchlight and siren. I carried our girl in her white blanket cocoon around
the corner of the house next door for a better look, and ice drenched my guts when
we ran into the moose coming back the other way across the mechanic's dandelion-crazed
lawn. I lurched for the sanctuary of the garage, thinking of how I'd killed our child

with good intentions, when a blast from the cop's siren
spooked the moose into the street
so that it skidded on the pebbly asphalt and slammed to the
ground with a jarring thud.
This was everything you missed. Except for the way the moose
loped off like a big
awkward kid down the alley under the pink and aquamarine
pulse of The Holiday
Theater's neon arrow, pursued by the cruiser, and the way I
stood in the driveway
with our baby girl and watched the mechanic and his wife and
son come out and stand
and watch, and how we looked at each other but didn't say
anything about how
even though we'd just witnessed a monumental ruckus things
were quieter than
they'd been in our neighborhood on a Saturday morning for a
long time.

My Six-year Old Daughter Rhapsodizes on the Food Chain in My Parents' Jacuzzi on Labor Day

Everywhere autumn has shot its first bolt of blue through the air. She grins while giving me a sing-song rundown about how everywhere the spider eats the fly, the frog eats the spider, the bird eats the frog, the cat eats the bird, the dog eats the cat, the bear eats the dog, and the shark eats the bear. A giant, she tells me, when I ask her who eats the shark. In the tepid murmur of chemical bubbles, our cosmos includes a red rubber octopus, a yellow rubber pelican, a black and white rubber killer whale, and a green rubber turtle. Someone has arranged five brittle robin nests across the back porch like the ages of humanity. They blaze in the still swordplay of white September sun. Everywhere a shark-headed giant sags in a backyard hammock of pale rope between two English hawthorns where he recites the taxonomy of our remaining daylight and waits to receive us with a yawn.

Uncle Steve Spontaneously Delivers a Miniature Lecture on the Nuances of Jungian Psychology on a Sunday Afternoon at Abbotsford

And although he's not my uncle but my mother-in-law's only brother, I still call him Uncle Steve outside the front entrance where, having driven in from Duns, he greets me. We chat idly about the ten years that have passed since he attended my wedding reception in Rochester. We watch two peacocks goose-step like spangled generals across the clipped green lawns. Just beyond, he tells me, would be the River Tweed, adding that the Scott home is in dire financial straits. And with a modest flourish he produces a business card from his wallet that shows his son is a Green Party MSP in Edinburgh. And he says his daughter is securing a grant to construct hedge mazes in Central Park as a public service. I fan out a brash panoply of snapshots: his niece, my wife of ten years, and our three daughters. At seventy-two, he remains unmarried to the woman he lives with. Before ambling off down the gravel path like a gray figure from fiction or history in his buff-colored cardigan and polyester slacks, he tells me that those women walk away from us with our *anima* in their hip pockets. And from the trees two peacock screams soar through the afternoon like love and death.

Poem Written After Visiting the Cumberland Pencil Museum in Keswick, Cumbria (I Want to Love You)

I want to love you in a way that's absurdly grand and impossible in its dimensions, the way I imagine Sonnet Man in his leather flying helmet and teal cape and tangerine tights, a big ABABCDCDEFEFGG on his chest, might wrench the world's largest pencil off the wall from under its official Guinness World Record plaque and hew cosmic-sized sentiments in the earth's beaches and red deltas, his words gouging up bees in amber and fossil thumbs of prehistoric lovers. I want to love you the way the boy Ben Franklin discovered he could sail across a lake with the string to a paper kite tethered to his knees. I want to stipple a sky of yellow kites above you with a landscape painter's ease.

I want to love you the way God paged Florence Nightingale under a tree in Embley Park, a simple summons to a lifelong quest, or the way Saturday eases into Sunday, beginning with a touchdown pass in the Alabama-Arkansas game and ending with a trio of house finches swarming the feeder like laughter and its afterthoughts.

But because love is no longer stylish and because I have come right out at the beginning and said I want to love you in so many amplified ways, perhaps a nervous impatience alone will stop people from reading the rest of this. Because I have used simple language and sought to be understood perhaps no one will call this poetry. It is precisely because I have not pretended to be writing from Tuscany or camouflaged my feelings behind wry allusions to pop culture or obscure nineteenth-century Polish philosophers, because I have not wrenched word meanings and syntax like a New Jersey bouncer twisting his girlfriend's arm into a chickenwing and shoving her into his Scirocco, that nobody will print this in a journal or read it in a magazine.

But even writing against agenda-driven poetry obsessed solely with technique is still writing with an agenda and a technique, especially since I began with a fanfare devoted to how I want to love you.

So perhaps all love poetry will always be a danger to itself, and the best thing would be not to write or say anything but simply to wait thirty years to lead you by the hand from the gaggle of paparazzi and Indonesian businessmen and women doing a half-dressed group karaoke to Carpenters tunes at the bar in the Turquoise Flamenco Internet Café out to an empty table on the piazza and silently observe how the penny-colored light of dusk bathing your profile reminds me of the sweeping wonder in all things as beautiful and epic as Ludwik Krzywicki's empiricocritical phenomenalism, or mountains and birds, or the rapture captured between capital letter and period, or the endless blue syllable of the Mediterranean sounding out all the ways I want to love you.

Matthew James Babcock

The Fall Olympics

Triple jumpers would leap into crisp heaps of frosty leaves.

Then the camera would cut to the windfall apple clean and jerk. In commercials, speed skaters would zip through orchards, plucking chilly plums and apricots. Sponsors from Münich and Sarajevo would circle campfires and roast whopping contracts.

Fencers would saw hickory, and volunteers in day-glo vests would lean against the rails, toying with ID lanyards and passing donuts and Styrofoam cups of spiced cider to teenagers in the smashing-mailboxes marathon. Cornstalks would be bundled Greco-Roman style.

All medals would be bronze.

Countries in temperate zones would crush world records while Sri Lankan committees scrimped to send a single long shot in second-hand mauve sweatpants to get trounced in the prelims of the pumpkin put.

All triumphs would be symbolic. All glory, mass decay. Scandal would mar international good will. Sabotaged starting blocks in the four-man storm window repair. Koreans in Dracula costumes caught blood-doping. Russians trained in Seattle would smuggle out secrets for synchronized weed burning.

In cruiserweight nostalgia, obscure triumphs would breed legends, if only in the life of the slouchy fifth-grade science teacher turned hardware-store owner who would remain undefeated for thirty years.

A volunteer shuttle bus driver, he would ferry a babblative gang of Belgian journalists and the Congolese rhythmic firewood chopping team through the venues and maple syrup stands to the athlete's village, north of Providence.

See his monkey forearms drape over the steering wheel, like a coach resigned to a sixth-place finish.

Now he squints and angles his head and beholds the throbbing glow of smoky autumn, and you are there among the hectic black overcoats and orange scarves, the red-nosed tourists and shopping bags crammed with souvenirs, the officials scurrying into coffee shops to escape the avalanche of fans, the incandescent plumes of thousands of human breaths under the streetlights, the cheerful Swedes crowding into Greek restaurants, elbow-to-elbow with the irascible back-up goalie for the Polish early snow polo team.

The look on his face tells you that he remembers it was on a Friday night in October, a night like this one after a college dance.

His voice drops with the weight of pleasure into a well of thick emotion as he retells it, and you see the two girls—one named Amy, and her roommate whose perfume smelled like peaches in bushel baskets—how they packed him in their royal blue Yugo, promising to catch air over the railroad tracks behind Interwest Cabinet.

You are in his memory.

You are his memory, his teammate sidelined with a sprain, cheering under your breath—*c'mon, c'mon*—watching the dreamy young man he was tail the girls like a dopey deputy across the park, shy, head down, hands in pockets, booting mounds of color-stained leaves: scorched russet, smudged olive, and robust gold ones that glow like footlights in the dewy night.

A baton flashes from his hand to yours, and a thrill revs in your belly, the engine that drives all desire.

In the back seat, girlish laughter squeals through switchbacks in your chest, and the fender strikes asphalt, spitting hot sparks, and when the front tires soar from a ski jump of darkness, you float like a body in love and are immortalized in a snapshot of history as cannons at the closing ceremony fire acrobatic crows into the twilight, and bats explode from a barn, glazed in orange moon, the air rushing from your lungs, not a gasp of joy, but the roar of hopefuls who have waited a lifetime for a chance in the race with loss.

The Transient Rains of April Thirteenth

If nothing else, I have this: I once saved a girl's life. Five years
back, before our son was born, I was walking a street that
had grown as familiar as your pulse. January. Twenty below.
Chestnut trees, stripped of their torches, hardened in the
fragile air. Crabapples blackened satchels of shriveled fruit. One
hundred and one mute crows whetted their feathers on the
bloodless sky. She wore frayed pajamas. Purple stripes. Her hair
bristled like the heart of winter. Her bare feet sloped down
driveway frost to the street. When she raised her arms to me, I
lifted the bundled cornstalks of her bones and took her to
the nearest house. You carry a stranger's child the way you
would deliver a pillar of carved glass. The way you carry
the angel fresco dislodged from the cathedral arch of your
remaining days. I knocked on a screen door. An older girl
answered, examined us through the ragbag curtain of her bangs.
Her brown T-shirt bore a jaguar face with emerald eyes.
"That's ours," she said, pushing the door open. Then *wump-*
wump-wump-wump. The mother's frantic stampede down
the stairs, her face an earthquake, and her arms gathering the
loose laundry of her daughter's soul to her breast. I walked
away, having learned something I would realize the day I stood
outside for the first time with our newborn son to taste the
glorious rain-gusts of spring: the faces of horror and ecstasy are
the same face. Later someone told me a black sickness had
stung the girl's mother the previous October—stage four cancer
was the offhand report—and now her face is the only thing
I see, now that the earth has grown as unfamiliar as your pulse,
and I swing our baby boy in the deadly basket of my arms

under April's unruly caravan of clouds, each boisterous plume a
mad crusade, the chill of fresh drops rallying blood in our
skin. I see the way she charged the threshold of her home,
snatched her golden hatchling from my outstretched arms,
and slammed the door as if I were not a hero but a terrible
disease.

Telos

My daughter, four years old, sits at a table in Miller Park across from the Rusty Parrot Lodge and lowers her cheeseburger long enough to say that babies turn into teenagers, and teenagers turn into parents, parents turn into grandparents, and then you die, right? Before I insist there's much more to it than that, I take a moment to observe the late afternoon sun draw itself across the opal mountains like a bow across cello strings

and wonder how many long eons of slow erosion it took for the gray-blooded stone parapets on the sagey hillsides to jut through, each wearing a smooth parliamentary scowl, like the Nez Percé warrior who must have slogged doggedly through elk as numerous

as the black flies on a grizzled hunk of carrion and, during the annual migrations to the summer grazing grounds on the shimmering switchbacks of the Gros Ventre River,

urged his son not to get down on himself if he didn't see the point of it all right away.

Matthew James Babcock

Sexual Limbo

Five months after our third girl is born, I rise from the sarcophagus of sleep and step into the hallway through the watery shroud of Saturday morning light to find I'm no longer living in a jerkwater Idaho town scudded with January slush but crouching

on a Caribbean island, my shoulders chapped with sunburn rosettes, the horrendous orange and red tartan of my clamdigger shorts clashing with a cloud of beard that dangles to my navel. The tropical air is tumid with coconut oil

and spindrift. Someone has pleached my beard with charms improvised from kelp and hermit crab shells. The limpid tattoo of a tambourine rides the gentle scroll of the surf, wafting from a smart catamaran on which four Harvard biology majors—two young men

and women whose parents have funded their vacation—toast each other with tequila shots. They trade fleeting glances of admiration for their thin, tan bodies banded in lime Speedos and ice-blue bikinis, then run a pink spinnaker up the main mast, which blooms

with the daiquiri-flavored trade winds of idle passion and bears their nimble pleasure craft past a mammoth cruise ship on which my wife lowers her shuffleboard rod, shields her eyes from the sea glare, and squints in my direction to see if it's me. Like porpoises of good omen,

our first two daughters surface through emerald waves, offering their backs as stepping stones, but the baby bobs between us on an orange waterskier's buoy, waving a warning in infant semaphore, and I shake off the risky notion of such a slippery traverse and return

to doodling in the sand with my big toe—a map of the cosmos I erase and scribble again a thousand times, each time producing the same pattern in the warm yellow silica. Years pass. A cantankerous anthropologist in a pith helmet doesn't unearth

the tangled archeology of my bones. Instead, it's tourists who flock each spring to decipher the fragments of old Beach Boys lyrics a madman has hewn with a mussel shell burin in lava rock monoliths of a man and women facing eastward. Another thousand years:

The statues give birth to a legend chanted by nude islanders during the jubilee blowfish hunt and fertility festival at summer solstice. Dusk glazes the ocean with amber fire, and the high priestess sings the ancient litany as her muscle-bound mate ravishes her

in an octagon of torches stabbed into the sand. The flickering glare dances down the slick backs of barking sea lions on the rocks, electrifies the stream of red juice she dribbles from a crushed pomegranate into his mouth. Our first mother and father, she sings,

bringers of each year's bountiful mackerel and banana harvest, pleased the gods the day they found this abandoned ivory tusk that after years of wise restraint and careful use shrank from the killer's knife they wielded to become the tiny polished amulet of power preserved and passed on through time to those generations of highest praise and honor.

This Story

There's this story my daughters keep asking me to tell them
at night. (The oldest is twelve, her younger sister, ten.)
It's about Gene, a kid who played on my baseball team.
When I tell it, Gene reappears in my mind,
where he'll always remain a rubber-jointed
freckle-pocked yokel on the stubbly playing fields behind the
Tupperware plant, a gangly
immortal slouching like a scarecrow
with a few struts yanked out, surrounded
by cow pastures, Styrofoam coolers, and chunky mothers
in rickety aquamarine lawn chairs,
the scorched odor of alfalfa and manure and the cheese factory
blowing across town.
(That year, my dad coached.
We were the Jerome Recreation District Rebels,
shirts and caps the color
of orange sherbet, bodies as unformed as after-school freedom).

Gene, because of his lanky stretch, was parked at first base.
I was the stocky two-bagger,
lurking deep in the pocket with a bushel-basket glove no line
drive could evade.
(Secretly, baseball terrified me. I feared the Bill Buckner
dribbler between the ankles,
the overthrow to first). Weekly, Gene and I drilled the
routine. I netted
every rocket grounder from a streak of torched grass.
My arm fired comets into Gene's dangling mitt. Over and
over, we practiced

the snappy out, waiting for game day to launch us into our
small-town cosmos of legends.

There's this umpire I remember, too. (Here the story diverges).
Scott Jackson.
Stork-legged, limber, and tan with a smoky storm of curls and
honey-colored mustache
that dripped from his upper lip, like a young Donald
Sutherland. (I'm thinking
of the early movies, *Kelly's Heroes* or *Animal House*, in which
he plays an apple-chomping, bedswerving Miltonist). The
thing I never told anyone is that sometimes I went to our
games
just to see Scott Jackson rumble up in his magenta Corvette
and lounge shirtless
on the hood in stringy cutoffs, his Ovation Balladeer angled like
his last girlfriend
across his lap as he sailed Cat Stevens over the batting cages into
the orange and purple
mayhem of sundown.

I idolized Scott Jackson because nobody with authority over me
would ever let me
live his life—one I imagined (and would later discover) that
involved temp jobs
in sleepy towns, bitter coffee in roadside cafés, romances as
unbridled and numerous
as tumbleweeds, and a diary crammed with cross-country
escapades

alongside our principal's son who had a PhD in folk songs
from some place in Virginia.
It didn't matter
that Scott Jackson umped in podunk interstate watering holes
so he could scrounge up
enough vending machine change to drag him through
Thursday. The scarred myth
of his presence was enough to keep me coming back to the
trampled ground we called
a diamond for another chance at the big play. (Here, my
daughters usually start nodding).

I'll always remember Gene because of one day. Scott Jackson,
the sun-roasted god,
crouched behind home plate. The batter for the A & W
Bobcats rapped a worm burner
toward second. With a nimble two-step, I scooped it from the
dirt and whipped it
to Gene.
(Now slow motion ensues). Through a film of violet light, the
ball arced like a loose moon
to first base. (The red stitches spun a frenzy of equators.) At
the same time, I saw
that Gene was not paying attention to the game. Cap askew,
buck teeth poking his chin,
he was gawking like a bonehead beaver, a reincarnation of
Mortimer Snerd, standing
on first base and turning his body back and forth, limp arms
flailing like straps

of cowhide nailed to a spinning post, oblivious to the play at
first, oblivious to life.

The ball struck him in the chest. His toothpick bones folded,
and he cried, "Ooph!"
The pink magician's handkerchief of his slack skin shot through
a slot to another dimension, leaving only
a flash of his blue sneaker soles.

It is when my daughters shake from slumber and laugh that I
don't say what I want to say.
(Mostly because I want them to savor happiness). What I
don't tell them is how
I understood instantly that hope for perfection destroys
another. In this story, I want
to tell them, the one you're living now, you will prepare for
years and when you find people who will stand and receive
your best, the love you hurl at them will cut them down
at the knees. This story, I want to say, the one you will trade
for the version
you will tell your children, is the one that makes a sport of joy
and, as long as we pass it on,
clinches our place in the endless game.

III

Heart and Root

Monody for the Modern World

Now Cicero Baptist Church inhabits Office Max.
Cattails dull the backswing of dawn's copper-bladed ax.

The diesel air sweetens arcs of stray killdeer distress.
Daylight scum drains culverts of a slag of silences.

Raven carols grate the sky like antiquated gears.
Gaunt shopfronts in plazas flake a prophecy of years.

Streaks of cloud on gravel rust the residue of night.
Dandelions unravel the next molecule of light.

Offramps tarnish pauses with a carbon caterwaul.
Stockstill geese bring forth broods at Burdick Auto Mall.

A cabaret of cars crowds Budget Inn and drive-thru.
A dash of finch and cardinal stains the elemental blue.

Erect a psalm to house a phase: absolute, absurd—
where a phrase of sun is manna and beginning is the word.

Matthew James Babcock

Reading up on the Qur'an in a McDonald's Playland

Thursday, after work I'm there,
my baby girl in a high chair.

My two older girls run pell-mell.
At home, my wife escapes her hell.

The hours until the last days lag.
Tobacco-colored college mag

tells me of vicegerent, Adam,
who leads devout Muhammadan

and cherub toddler, French fry-fed,
down corkscrew slide of doomsday red.

Other fathers don't spare a glance.
We contemplate deliverance.

Through the drive-thru, slick with grime,
pickups haul the soul sublime.

I issue silent fatwas to
the kids whose noses run with goo,

who, cold-infected, smeared with sin,
put brimstone hands to my babe's chin.

I think of that Apocalypse—
the sky as scarlet as clown's lips.

Will my girls rally in the flame?
Will stern Allah pronounce my name

as destroyer of death's angel
or dub me Daddy Infidel?

I see us, hands linked, tumbling through
a zigzag crawl tunnel of blue.

Our food goes cold. The fire grows hot.
Spring snow adorns the parking lot.

We drive home. The earth strips away.
The sky's light falls like Judgment Day.

Matthew James Babcock

Running in Stratford

I would rather be running in Stratford
than driving westward on County Line Road
to the town of Grant for a spaghetti
fundraiser under a cast-iron sky
from which frail November snowfall dwindles
like campfire ash in eleven degrees.
The girl I know who set the price at three
bucks a plate, when she woke and untangled

herself from the mangled heap of her two-
ton to find the baby in the other
car died, must have wished to don winged track shoes
and go until she reached the foam-smothered
Avon, stopping to stretch where dirty swans
smudged with sunlight turn drugged revolutions
in the rainbow scum on the still water.
I see us all running. Take my daughter's

first-grade teacher, who moved from Washington
to read *Amelia Bedelia* and wait
for a transplant for her husband, two sons
at home. I see them—ill and overweight—
limbering up in shorts of pink Spandex,
numbers safety-pinned, the sunken matchbox
of Hall's Croft the site for the starter's gun
at the To-Be-Or-Not-To-Be Fun Run.

No matter who you are, you leave your room
at The Quilts & Croissants before sunrise
in battered cross-trainers, finding a pace

in the fine ecclesiastical thrum
of the rain outside Holy Trinity.
In the country, splashes from tall nettles
lash you across the chest, and certainly
you think that if you do not feel your pulse

or stop to check your watch you can outrun
your sister-in-law dead from cancer at
thirty-eight, an unwanted gay obscene
phone call your first year at college, or that
time Delfin Ordaz said he'd kick your ass
outside PDQ Chicken 'N' Taters.
Late into the afternoon renaissance
of your life, your third lap around The Swan,

your grief becomes a young understudy
who, unshaven and unkempt, leaves bloody
thoughts and rhetoric for a smoke break on
the back rail—where French schoolkids in gold caps
and Dutch retirees lean and toss bread scraps
from box lunches to ducks—squints at the sun,

then steps back through the stage door to rehearse
for a *Dog in the Manger* matinée,
the offhand energy in his flat words
telling a story that spans from today

to a Golden Age when your pain and mine
stepped to the footlights and spoke its first line.

Matthew James Babcock

Running in Mullaghmore

Today, I escape the humid crypt
of The Beach Hotel and beat
a script of rippled footprints across
the strand of nautilus gray and tan,
my trail unrolling a Gaelic riddle
indecipherable to all except
a staunch parliament of ruddy cows
as impassive as a century of dawns.

Pacing sky, I lace feet and ankles
in traces of saltwater spindrift,
scare seagulls from tide pool rocks,
skip the sandy skiff of my tracks
across the barnacle spine of the earth
long enough to outlast and outpace
the age of fishing trawlers whose
rusted hulls sag in the breakwater
and transcribe time as a colossal wreck.

The race is always to leave everything
behind. The gravel caterwaul
of campaign slogans from bullhorn
and pub, reedy bluff where
river invokes ocean, white flux
of gold-leaf glare on morning surf
from whose scrolls of sluggish thunder
cormorants scatter with elegant force
in spirals of black flight designed
not to find speed but a divine place.

Sextina

Our neighbor, frowzy and born again, enshrined
herself in knickknacks of rainbow grace
and rammed a revved vacuum cleaner
against her apartment wall to mask
our repertoire of moans: Jesus Saves!
The naked plaster flaked like old pottery.

Teenage dad-to-be downstairs crowded poetry
in the margins of Chili Peppers tablature, entwined
his rangy Mr. Gas attendant's body, live,
in his blond girlfriend's. In the blue-grays
of midnight they danced an angry masque
around our parked car in the clean air.

Afternoons were dreams picked clean. Our
summer words summoned a sleepy coterie
of fables. October saw Needham Mansion masked
in armor frost; at noon, butterscotch suntanned.
The old depot simmered Café Habañero grease
the year we drove back to where we lived.

I remember the chuckle of firestarter leaves
under a blanket on which we lay, cleaner
from a lake swim. Our flint-and-steel hips grazed
the ground in the forest's primeval Godwottery
of lichen rust and root, our skin sap maple-and-pined.
Over the water, the sun lowered a red mosque.

We turn territorial. We roam. Ask
yourself how present love refracts though sieves
of fact the patchwork past. Settled couple, unbound
under laundered duvet, sighs and reclines, or
slumps on pawnshop mattress like jittery
newlyweds transported in serial *coups de grâce*.

Three children now. I stray where the cattail grows
in palatine clumps and bindlestiff musk-
rats gnaw frozen garbage in the watery
January fade. Glossolalia from waxwings on the *qui vive*
for goldeneyes in loose ellipses on the clamor
of the black river praises the way your clothes unwind.

Over and over, desire finds the torrent enshrined
in a mask of ice. The vagitus of spring shatters
the ancient pottery with a cleaner grace that saves.

Sunnet

Old roses they can't sell at Everyday
Floral make fresh gifts for the elderly.
Parking is scarce outside the nursing home.
We bear slack bouquets through a smoke-free zone.
Inside, souls wilt. Outside, jackhammers bray.
A bonfire of blossoms trims the backbone
of the Beaverhead Mountains. The March moon
warms its ball of fluorescent ice in sky.
Supernovas, now black buds in thorny
baskets of stars, released their crimson gloom
the day Columbus sailed. Their afternoons
we crush like petals in grooved palms of clay.
A beautiful grief not worth our crying.
All light that strikes is already dying.

Matthew James Babcock

Sapphics for Brugge

After a crisp crab-salad baguette lunch on
a sun-warped bench along the Mariastraat,
I got in to see the *Madonna met Kind*,
    swarmed by Japanese

whose windbreakers of cavalier pink and orange
and chattering cameras clashed with the stone
arches and silence. I scooted over for a
    tour group from Dumfries.

The finely scooped folds of Carrara marble
coaxed my hand to reach out and confirm them cloth
even after I strolled through the exit door,
    considered the ease

with which memory proceeds a true longing.
Belgian glare struck the cobbles like stained glass as
I walked back on foot and in mind, recalling
    the Dover ferries

to Calais, squads of gulls scrolling sad circus
cries behind on broad invisible ribbons
of sea air. Becket lay—before this woman,
    stone child on her knees—

in Canterbury, his martyrdom fused with
my thoughts of what it would be like to have
a shrine set up for some nine hundred years on
    the spot your breath ceased.

Or you—in the maternity wing of a
county hospital, sculptors and sage pilgrims
trekking there for decades to hail events as
    glorious as these.

Matthew James Babcock

All This for a Dollar

The town sex offenders hibernate
in faded houses of sunshine and grit.
Late February's rusted coffee can
of loose change casts its tarnished glare
against the unwashed windows
of Honk's $1.00. A Sacajawea coin
from my pocket buys my daughter
one Saturday morning of transcendence.

In sweatshirt and jeans, I am gyrovague
among plungers and notepad ladybugs.
Her pilgrimage transports her, hair unbrushed,
past sports drinks and loofahs. The sleepy
dharma of grapefruit squirt bottle
and gravy boats lulls Christopher Cross
and James Taylor through labyrinths of cheap
candle scents: Pearberry Jam, Victorian Petal.

Her ardor is such I hesitate
to criticize her quest. Just wait,
I want to say. Life will peddle you
Easter candy on President's Day. Expiration
dates will leer like seedy sailor tattoos
from wrinkled bags of stuffed jalapeno
chips. You will swap youthful expeditions
after the Ur Knick Knack for the daily news.

Her selection, a warped glass vase
for her mother, finds the bright underside
of my stance on the drive home:
Still, Jenny, 11.5-inch fashion doll, could
flip the brassy foil sun from her thumb
and land you—heads or tails—as
a suntanned member of the Sweet Memories
picture frame family, or Indian princess

guiding explorers with a new world voice
to which assorted penguin figurines,
having hobbled off dusty shelves,
will march from sweatshops in the Philippines
across the porcelain Antarctic, half-starved,
if only for the thrill of living with a choice
and bypassing a five-and-dime rival
in tireless pursuit of the bargain of survival.

Matthew James Babcock

TALK SHOW

You gotta show me you love me, uh uh,
she shouts. *Ain't no good just to say it.* The
host sports a cheap Hawaiian blouse, agrees,
proffers roving mic to both families.
Everyone gestures. Words are not enough.
From my barber's chair perch, it's a circus:
a T.V. screen of hands, grins, oohs and ohs
for a bulimic mom, son they called "goof."
In this shop's hall of mirrors, they become
fat lady, ringmaster, strongman, clown, bum.
The Nam vet giving me a trim looks bored.
He lowers his scissors, acts out his words:
"Them things'll come back like a boomerang."
(As if to demonstrate what he's saying).

Embrace, Backlit

Tourist Information Stop, Highway 89, Logan Canyon, January 1995

No brown tree trunks, my photographer friend
said, *if you look. Just black, ash, lichen-toned.*
His hypothesis finds itself tested
where two teenagers hug each other, dressed
warmly, a slate-gray elm in the picture.
She's unfocused, wears a look like winter.
He remains rapt, doesn't want her to go.
Mittened hands probe her spine, and I see how
we see through things and what things seem to be
as they develop little eye-to-eye.
A moment, and they're gone. And gradually,
it becomes clear that their love stays undone
under charcoal limbs that never grasped sky,
that holding's not the same as holding on.

Matthew James Babcock

NOVEMBER BURN

The paper souls of poplar leaves
  ascend through cloudless glare.
The charred pieces trace helices
  of ancient sky and air.

Rain liberates the captured spark.
  Dry riverbeds combust.
Wind lassos in its razor arc
  the kingfisher's exodus.

Late day, late hour. Orange coals wane
  in the ash of sodden scars.
The ruddy earth's black map of veins
  grows brittle as the stars.

The landlocked man remains at dusk,
  clothes soaked in smoked perfume.
Blood smolders in the withered husk
  of luminescent gloom.

Visions at Birch Creek

Albert Lyons, teamster, escaped Nez Percé slaughter
where my freckled ten-year-old daughter
with borrowed Eagle Claw pole casts in
for brook trout whose quicksilver combustion
flashes like the stolen mule-train firewater
Chief Joseph drank under sky everlasting.

Blood marks the rendezvous by degrees.
Throbbing gills. The imminence of her menses,
river of no return. And western tanagers, red-
orange skulls drenched in sunrise shades,
fleet incarnations of luckless Chinese
who took Nee-Me-Poo hatchets to the head.

One wonders how Albert survived. Did he too
hallucinate on air? Did he plunge hands into
prism currents for fish mirages, having
flitted through the willows from liquor-loving
braves along the bottoms? Did he crawl *pari passu*
with unborn daughters under war-paint evening?

The savage moment bids us be women and men.
We stand by to be butchered or else stun
lacerated knees and chapped palms in a daze
on prairie shale and sage. Let the tanager blaze
of my daughter's hair consume the whiskey sun.
Let our presence outlast the massacre of days

long enough to inhabit ghost-town hotel and shack.
Too large to keep, too small to throw back.

Matthew James Babcock

Anniversary

Ten years later she takes me back
to Mandarin Garden Chinese Restaurant

where in the frayed ruby light
of greasy tissue lanterns we trade platitudes

like *Time really flies* and *We've been gone*
overnight, but it feels like forever

over Tiny Spicy Chicken and Buddha's Pork.
The frail paper placemat says she's

the Ox, given to patience and persistence,
an ideal match for me, the Cock,

selfish and eccentric, advised to avoid Rabbits.
Outside, the noon traffic on Main Street

drones into gleaming future and past
through ticker-tape flakes of snow

shaken from the balcony of November sky,
each peak in the Wellsville Mountains

a guest strapped in high collar and cravat.
On the return drive, we lapse into wordlessness.

Milestones: hitchhiker in lime green anorak.
Skeletal Ford chassis in a field.

Handmade signs reading *Garden of Eatin'*
and *Free Idaho: Repeal Right to Work.*

A scrap of black plastic garbage sack
snagged on a music staff of barbed wire

flaps a one-note anthem in the crosswind.
At the Bonneville County line, a ring-necked pheasant

springs up from roadside scrub brush
the color of husks, a spindly Peking acrobat

in harlequin silks and sash somersaulting
through the next decade's hoop of fire.

She watches, asks about next year's plans.
I squint ahead at where the road vanishes

into the zodiac of what remains, where in
the hub of the wheel Buddha sits

in a blond pasture on a shattered stump,
weaving slipknot paradoxes about

the Ox—tender and prone not to slack,
plodding on forever to arrive overnight—

and the Cock, perched on her back,
keenly observant of time's stationary flight.

Matthew James Babcock

American Paradelle for Dublin

These streets parallel a place I've been before.
These streets parallel a place I've been before.
I could wait for you and find waiting a wonder.
I could wait for you and find waiting a wonder.
I've been waiting for a place before these streets.
Wait, and I could find you a parallel wonder.

Pigeons the color of newspaper flutter outside Trinity.
Pigeons the color of newspaper flutter outside Trinity,
and they wrap themselves in tatters of wind.
And they wrap themselves in tatters of wind.
Outside, they flutter, wrap themselves in tatters of color—
the trinity of pigeons, wind, and newspaper.

The blank day wanes in a smoke of hours.
The blank day wanes in a smoke of hours.
Your clock tower glances mark time and space.
Your clock tower glances mark time and space.
Your day wanes. Space and time tower in a clock.
Blank glances of smoke mark the hours.

The streets outside parallel a trinity: time, space, and …
They wrap a day for themselves in tatters of hours.
The blank color of pigeons and newspaper wanes
in wind. Find your place. Before you
wonder and these glances flutter, mark a clock tower
of smoke. I could wait. I've been waiting.

Cherry Tomatoes: A Rhapsody

The taste of the tang and the taste buds themselves.
A barb-lipped encounter. An impulse unshelved.

Taut nipples. Tongue tip stippled with eloquence
inarticulate. Tripped-up triple-time dance.

Copland brass on the radio while driving.
Waiting for you at the airport: Wyoming.

Bitter bonfire. Heart and root. Cinder of day.
Stem snapped off while green. Saved, thrown away.

Carnation mob erupting, stabbing the light.
Scorched flavor. Orb of lava. Part torch, part fruit.

The slant of sundown through a line of laundry.
Gray loam scrounged under fingernails, gone dry.

None to show how the bloodshot September moon
smolders on the butte—fuscous, incarnadine.

Cosmos of burst flame, the seed planets deranged.
Raw and round the routine. Restless life unchanged.

IV

Spare Changes

The History of the World

There is not a single History of the World
—Whitman

Even with thirteen years in The Bloody Tower,
how did Ralegh think he could
get it all down in
his *History of the World*? Somewhere
between The Ice Age and William Langland

you're bound to omit something.
Whether it's King Cnut or Old Sarum,
you'll drop the ball somewhere for sure.
Even the most astute historian runs the risk
of skipping trilobites or flint knapping,

as thoughtful he rises from
his yellow borderware chamber pot
and returns to the incomplete treatise ablaze
under trembling canopies of pink candlelight
on an oak writing desk in the corner.

Retrieving his quill, he launches
into tobacco trade routes and the bluestones
of Stonehenge, excluding in that moment
a thumbnail sketch of the Flemish artisan whose
circuit-board tapestry adorns the cell's north wall.

On closer scrutiny the whole prospect
is peppered with logistical snags.
Consider the question of what's versus why's.
For instance, your history might
touch on *The Martyrdom of St. Sebastian*

but not say why he looks so sublimely pleased
on the museum wall, a criss-cross salvo
of crossbow bolts shot through his torso.
Nor would it offer commentary on the Granny Smith
apple I finished after turning from poor Seb

and wandering away, the padded clank
of the chewed core in the trash can outside
the café in the National Gallery, the tart pendant
on the bare wall of my throat a ripe epilogue
to the moment. Nor would your history

present a summary of these thoughts, the ones I've
scribbled here, which while trivial to some
still comprise a scrap of the world's history.
So no history can
be called the world's history.

Even if you tried, outright obsolescence would be
the best you could achieve.
On the golden April afternoon
you snugged the kerning
and polished the margins and pagination

you'd be finished as a writer
in the same instant
you failed to include all the bright blue humdrum
events that happened on the day you boxed
your manuscript and shipped it to your publisher's

New York office with a cirrus cloud
like a laughing Scottie dog easing across
the slipstream of Tuesday,
two charcoal cats footloose in your untrimmed
arbor vitae, the paperboy hiccupping past your study

window on his yellow moped. After madness
drove you to your grave,
a nagging infinity would pursue
time's remnant where a morose
semicircle of scholars on pilgrimage—

abundant blossoms brightening
their hands like the colors of rain—
huddled in solemn tribute on the muddy plot
facing your tombstone in a local cemetery
in an obscure Montana mining town

where you listed onto the hard shoulder
in a rental car, trying to fathom
how to type faster in order to record events
before they happened—minutiae never
to be serried in any addendum or index.

So here's to the real history of the world:
excursus on skinned knees and foil gum wrappers
in pockets, the unwritten saga whose subtext
chronicles coughs in fifth-grade classrooms,
leaky Laotian fruit barges and forced apologies

on Wall Street subways, graham cracker crumbs,
the fables in blades of grass, the songs
of regret slogging through sullen strangers
on rainy days in foreign countries,
the exact tally of ice water refills

performed in Italian restaurants,
and extravagant bouquets of old newspapers
blown with pigeons and McDonald's milkshake cups
from benches across Piccadilly Circus.
In the history of the world, volume eleven thousand

sixty-two, page four, right hand column,
middle of the second paragraph from the top,
I'll always be leaning from a second-story window
over the traffic-jam nocturne
that lazes like an electric centipede in the rain

down London's Warwick Way, my shirt
collar unbuttoned, a gloss of cool sweat
swelling like dusk on my forehead, unable to name
the breed of songbird whose jubilant fanfare
ascends in buoyant strands and volleys

over the bent TV antennae and charred chimneys
atop the Surtees Hotel, the carved urban music
rising like the honed arrow shafts
of infant cries that will pierce
my wife across the Atlantic when our daughter

is born into the prison of the here and now,
where no iron-filing ink strikes calfskin vellum and no
devoted scribe's hand with gold-leaf paint
starts chapter and verse where she's scholar and saint.

Matthew James Babcock

The Thing I Don't Understand

the thing I don't understand about some contemporary
educational approaches to poetry
is why they put pictures
in the books,

        and all the questions they ask

   and see,   well,

        I don't recall I've always felt this way
but when they put me as a substitute teacher in Mr. Emmett's
     English 9B class, room #2, down the
hall

                    I started out
                    feeling stupid
                    then sorry

                            (at 1:25 pm the kids shuffled in,
     dragging bookbags, headphones jackhammering

                                        music in their ears, and all I
     could think was: ragtag, motley, harlequin, psychedelic)

they, as directed by their teacher, had to read poems
and answer study questions in their book: ***Understanding***
     Literature

                                (there was a picture on the front
     cover, an impressionistic

bridge
spanning
a blurred river.

Van Gogh's *Sunflowers*
was

in the hall too, I noticed)

there were three sections
assigned
to each poem:

STUDY QUESTIONS

Recalling

1. List the images of nature the poet uses to describe his feelings about his world. How many can you find?

2. In the last line, there is a specific reference to an animal. Are there any other references to animals? List them.

3. The poem is in the form of a conversation. Try and determine who is speaking to whom and write down as many scenarios as you can. (i.e. Mother to Son, Father to Son, Groom to Horse, etc.)

Interpreting

4. The poet writes that "heaven goes galloping, thrice journeyed onward." In what way does the poet intermingle the concrete with the abstract, and how does this affect the reader's impressions?

5. What does the poet's emphasis on animals tell you about his relationship with the natural world?

Extending

6. Think back to your last summer vacation. Did you see any animals? Write a short paragraph about the animals you saw, the things they did, and the way you felt about them. If you like, you may try to put it in the form of a poem. Consider concrete details, for example, the way they smelled, where you saw them, and what noises they made, if any. Include as many sensory details as you can and try to sum up how it changed any previous notions about animals you may have had.

yeah, great

so

they started working (some with headphones on, some with
 them off)

   and a girl,
way
in
the
back
 raises her hand and asks if they have to write in complete
 sentences

and I say, yes, they have to write in complete sentences, and
 then Ruen Duong (seating chart)
 asks if they have to do Extending, and I say, yes, they have
 to do Extending, and Celeste Urrea

  shoots her arm up
in a Nazi salute and says, uh-uh, that's wrong, he never makes
 us do Extending, you don't know what you're
talking about, he never makes us do Extending
 and I say, look, just do
 Extending,

      okay? Just do Extending, he didn't
 write anything about *not* doing Extending on the lesson
 plan, so just do Extending, do it all, and write in complete
 sentences

   it ain't gonna

kill ya

so class ends, finally,

and I wave goodbye to Ruen Duong,

to Celeste Urrea,

headphones clap
over their ears

and a kid named Avery Baines

lingers long enough
to tell me
(thank you, Avery)

that
it's no fun
when

you

dis/sect

a po-

em. that you should just read it

(he stapled

his assignment

[*ka-*

chunk] and

let it

flutter
to the
desk) and left

but I wanted to stop him
and say, Avery

Avery, I wanted to say (watching him shuffle out

the

door

Avery, you know, that's
what

I
think, Avery, that's a cool name

A v e r y B
a i n e s

A
v
ery Bain
es

a very b
aines

and Avery
Baines, you know sometimes I don't

know
why they call it *Understanding Literature*
when there's
nothing

to understand, really,

just things to feel,
experience,

just things   to   see

And oh, Avery Baines,

Avery Baines, baby, Avery Baines, buddy, you unkenneled the
monster this morning, mister,

because

sometimes I don't care
(I don't think anyone does)

about what I can Recall from a poem
or what I can Interpret

in
a
poem
and you know it's true I couldn't give a horse's most times,
anyway

but the Extending, Avery, always do the Extending,

that's what's so important: the Recalling, the
Interpreting, they can
take a
hike
on a
bike

but the Extending, no that's different
always do the
Extending, because

that's where poetry
happens:

poetry is Extension

and most times, what you'll
find is that

what you understand

won't
help
you.

in fact, what people think they understand tends to
get them

in trou-
ble. So, what I'm saying, Avery Baines, pal,

Avery Baines, man of the hour on the tower of
a power shower,

is always do the Extending, go for the Extending

and don't always think poetry
is
about
understanding.

Because, Avery Baines, sometimes if you really want to know

I think that poetry
(like a lot of things)
approaches me
more than I approach
it.

because if we're not careful, Avery Baines, if you and I
eventually get our noses out of the

foggy blue textbooks

for
once

if we
dogear the hazy pages, shut them,   mark our places

                                        and take a look
    a-   round

we just might bump into the world
one day,

                        (having read enough about things without
    experiencing them)

        and meet somewhere

and our conversation
might take

the form of a poem—

    it might *give*
                                        the form of a poem,

and impressions might
strut into our lives
                                    into our minds
                like   freewheeling sunflowers on parade

                                        and you'll see, and this, in part, is
    what I'm trying to say, Avery Baines,

You'll get the impression, among other
things, that

sunflower

is part
sun and
flower,

that sometimes the sun isn't necessarily the
sun,
that a flower isn't always a flower, that the sun blooms, and
flowers radiate

and that
at
the level of the word itself, two
distinct things

can join to form a third unique thing

and all
this at the level of the word spoken, the word written.

and this will be the biggest truckload of education you'll ever
get, Avery Baines, I'm telling

you,
seriously,

that the questions they ask,
aren't
as important as the questions
You ask

You'll blur borders
and
build rivers where there were

bridges.

You'll find so many that you can't list them (the natural world is
part animal and human)
I wouldn't
lie about something like this.
and we might even spend considerable time on why they put
pictures
in poetry books, and

I, Avery Baines, I
might quote
how a picture is worth a
thousand words

and You might say, yes, but

one word is
worth a thousand worlds
and, Avery Baines, if we're not careful

what I'm saying,

                                        what this is all about,
                                         is   1. if I Extend myself

2. and You Extend
Yourself

if we're
            not careful

3. it might happen:

someday, somewhere

                                                      we might
                                                                                  end
     up
4. sitting down

5. and asking each other questions,   even if I die

years before   you   do, continents apart,
                                                  the ocean rifts and
        volcanic trenches our only lifeline,

6. we might
end
up
meeting (if only on the page)
            and sitting down and
talking about the thing You don't understand, the thing I don't
     understand.

Inch

For do you not see how everything that happens
keeps on being a beginning
—Rilke

Three daughters harvest handfuls of inchworms
in the back yard where their mother played as
a girl. Each slim green acrobat twists, squirms,
and rappels down its fine silver essence
through the clean risk of air to be cupped in
hands, clapped in storage jars of criss-crossed grass,
the clear lids of Press 'N' Seal cellophane
pierced with fork holes. I speed with it all past
the Dansville Foster-Wheeler plant, Cuba
Coachlight Motel, and Arkport's Hurlbut House,
the medieval hills of Pennsylvania
and New York scrolling along faceless hours
of state highway that link my then to now.
And the world is different where I go.

And the world is different where I go
past the township of Friendship, toward Challenge,
miles from Desire and Panic. The hot orange
flare of oriole speed zigzags solo
between trees split with bronze gashes of sun.
Pale summer dapples ponds with a pollen
as thin as mist. Lily pads worship light.
This is the farthest off I have felt—right
now—and the closest I have come by far.
Pinpoint gnats of citrus fire wheel and spar.
The mind snags sticky filaments. The land
clutches the same daylight that fills the jar.

I spool the emptiness around a strand
of soul. There is little we understand.

Of soul, there is little we understand
or parcel out, collect in increments,
the intervals of dusk, glide and descent.
You envision the Seneca crop planned
to perfection here like a loose grid of
stars. The Cornplanter families, one half
in slack semicircles, busily scraped
the bark from red shoots to brew emetics.
The other half stared and traced the complex
theorems of random time and space that would
one evening find spoons of beveled dogwood
and the warped shafts of handmade arrows trapped
in the hard gray mud of love's fossil fern
where thoughts like cloud turrets form and reform.

Where thoughts like cloud turrets form and reform,
noon slants through the college café windows.
The room reels like a stock market forum.
A decade before he drives all those slow
miles to restart his life—a caravan
of native narratives interwoven
with the glimmering tableaux of their three
young girls scampering, arms upraised, to claim
chartreuse worms descending on light beams—
he sits near her and says nothing when she
breaks into his thoughts and life with a word.
He rises, wishes later he'd said more.

They leave. They meet again. Children follow.
The infinite starts and stops with hello.

The infinite starts and stops with hello.
The manner of birth confirms this to them.
First girl: born late on the Susquehanna;
tears the nipple from her mother's full breast;
December moon and skin jaundice yellow;
stork bites; head of hair a razzmatazz flame;
a brusque nurse who stays past her shift, and a
twenty-two hour battle with little rest.
The rictus of pleasure and smile of pain
trade places after hours. Laugh becomes scream.
Dark day and white night cycle in sun-stain-
and-star-smeared circuits of dawn-soaked streams
of curtains too tattered for them to rend.
Beginning begins beginning to end.

Beginning begins beginning. To end
is to deny the circle's open source.
Second girl: a pixie stalk of wheat-blond
that sprouts from the arid banks of the south
fork of the Teton. Sidesteps chance death twice.
One afternoon, the weekend of the Fourth,
north of the township of Sempronius,
he bolts toward the hummingbird feeder poles
across a lakeside cabin's deck and yanks
her back before she falls into a creek's
rocky ravine. Later, she survives an
occluded lung pipe, convalesces on

cherry popsicle sighs and gravel moans
just as ending draws the last starting line.

Just as ending draws the last starting line
another strand ravels out like the first
two. Third girl: August-born, like her mother
and sister, a gaze of retrospection,
wide-eyed and sublime, drama unrehearsed.
She keeps them both searching forward rather
than back—atonal carousel laughter
and calliope grins and three stitches
laced across a slender red slash that rips
open her temple like delicate lips
promising a kiss fourteen years after.
At Tubman's grave, the camera catches
her first steps. On moss-mad stone snail trails sketch
a glinting line or circle. Which is which?

A glinting line or circle which is, which
was, and which will be intersects the arc
of days upstate near the Erie Canal
and the home of Susan B. Anthony.
The girl who will one day chase a spry batch
of girls around her house and city park
loves a terrier named Duke and enrolls
in after-school ballet, earns mad money
waitressing summers at The Bluewater.
When asked for a portrait of love and home,
she sits a little more erect, recalls
the stuffed bear from her dad, how he pulled her

in a sled after a lakefront snowfall.
The moment remains more timeless than time.

The moment remains more timeless than time,
untraceable, like 1969,
when his folks bring him, as a newborn, back
from San Francisco's St. Luke's. Zodiac
Killer shoots a cabby. A maverick mutt,
Tasha, all morning and night, barks and trots
above their cheap crackerbox apartment.
He remembers the folklore glamor of
Buffalo Springfield's bassist getting bent
into a hood ornament as one half
of a head-on motorbike-and-bus crash.
It takes ten years after graduation
for life to find him in another town
that delivers forever in a flash.

That delivers forever in a flash.
This extends minutes to millennia.
First night alone, after the mania
of the reception, a drunk guest bangs harsh
encores of "Chopsticks" in the no-host bar
downstairs at The Sherwood Inn. It's not far
to the pier where they huddle in the gray
shriek of a November gale. They are kids
wrapped in college sweatshirts and hope. Now they
can live off whatever brummagem love
they might dump in handfuls under the lid
of a souvenir mug on a back shelf

with orphan dice, thumbtacks, and spare changes.
Earth forms as much as it rearranges.

Earth forms as much as it rearranges
us. Each lakeside autumn tree exchanges
the cutthroat blaze of monarch drapery
for a skeleton of stripped ebony.
The buzzsaw string quartets of cicadas
drown the spluttering cough of an outboard.
Seagulls grapple. Red deer ascend above
the corn. Boats get stored in dry dock. A hard
plane of gray-green ice mars the shore. It is
the blue heron's basso lament that moves
locals to mourn the influx of resort
kitsch. Headstones bloom. Cafés fold. As strange as
the passage of days, the long age cuts short
the connection between us, whose range runs.

The connection between us, whose range runs
to the blind limit of sense, marks milestones
on the stretched strand of light: The Hofbräuhaus;
Lindisfarne; Aran; Woody's Island; close
to breaking past Rock Springs; Promontory;
Balanced Rock; Moab; no guts, no glory
in Sturgis; lost in Blyth, if nothing else;
thunder and woodchucks at Buttermilk Falls;
Stonehenge's cold, sun-scoured palms; The Hub;
the grassy stone bowl of Old Sarum; dab
of Belgium; gig in Nagoya; beebalm
at Yellow Creek; between commitments at Bear

Lake; sunrise in Honduras sending psalms
head to tail, the span of cosmic measure.

Head to tail, the span of cosmic measure,
plots my observations now where I'm found.
I believe there's no isolation more
exquisite than the hours that course around
Fairman's Family Laundromat tonight.
A lone girl smokes and sits cross-legged in
parking space A18, her broken pane
hairstyle bleached the frightening opal-white
of summer lightning. Though I would say that
she has buckled fate's studded dog collar
around herself, I know we both spin out
of our bellies the frailest lifelines, our
hands cupped for the curious blood of what
we're caught in as prisoner and treasure.

We're caught in, as prisoner and treasure,
this escape and release. A memory: Cheyenne.
Midday, we pulled off to gas up the car
at a truck stop whose name I've forgotten.
A smog of slate rain draped saturated
murals on the ranks of boxcars, their mustard
broadsides spangled in angry comic-strip
swarms of pink-orange graffiti from Rocky Top
to Los Angeles. The wheels clanked and screeched
in a way that said *Gather* and *Always*
move on—not in light years but by the inch.
And pause often en route to clear the way

for roadblocks, and for visions and lunch where
three daughters harvest handfuls of inchworms.

Three daughters harvest handfuls of inchworms,
and the world is different. Where I go,
of soul, there is little we understand.
Where thoughts like cloud turrets form and reform,
the infinite starts and stops with hello.
Beginning begins, beginning to end,
just as ending draws the last starting line,
a glinting line or circle. Which is which?
The moment remains more timeless than time
that delivers forever in a flash.
Earth forms as much as it rearranges
the connection between us, whose range runs
head to tail, the span of cosmic measure
we're caught in as prisoner and treasure.

Acknowledgments

Alehouse: "Sextina"
Blue Lyra Review: "The Fall Olympics"
"Sexual Limbo"
Boxcar Poetry Review: "Kissing Booth: Twenty-Seven Years Later"
Burningword: "Junior Gymnastics Karma"
"Statistics from My Daughter's Sixth Grade Choir Concert"
decomP: "Threnody for an Idaho Spring"
Florida English: "Idaho Etude: 1"
"Idaho Etude: 2"
Foundling Review: "Miniature Golf Karma"
Heartlodge: "Telos"
High Horse: "Mittelschmerz"
HOOT: "Talk Show"
Irreantum: "Anniversary"
"Jerusalem Artichoke"
"Visions at Birch Creek"
"Nostalgia for Teenagers"
"The Spring Olympics"
The Laughing Dog: "Embrace, Backlit"
The Literary Bohemian: "Sapphics for Brugge"
Lake Effect: "Running in Mullaghmore"
Light: "November Burn"
Lucidity: "Reading up on the Qu'ran in a McDonald's Playland"
Mixed Fruit: "Lima"
Other Voices: "Cherry Tomatoes: A Rhapsody"

PANK: "The Transient Rains of April Thirteenth"
Poecology "Idaho Etude: 3"
"Idaho Etude: 4"
"Idaho Etude: 5"
Poetry for the Masses: "All This for a Dollar"
Poetry Super Highway: "Reunion"
Prime Number: "The History of the World"
Psychic Meatloaf: "Even Now"
Quiddity: "The Way My Three-year Old Daughter Runs Naked through the House Early Wednesday Evening"
Rattle: "Passage"
Sand: "American Paradelle for Dublin"
"Sunnet"
San Pedro River Review: "Five Laotians"
Spoon River Poetry Review: "Running in Stratford"
Staccato: "My Six-Year Old Daughter Rhapsodizes on the Food Chain in My Parents' Jacuzzi on Labor Day"
Stringtown: "Saturday Bike Ride (Unity of the Self)"
Terrain: "Moose Remembered"
"Poem Written after Visiting the Pencil Museum in Keswick, Cumbria (I Want to Love You)"
"Uncle Steve Spontaneously Delivers a Miniature Lecture on the Nuances of Jungian Psychology on a Sunday Afternoon at Abbotsford"
Yes, Poetry: "Monody for the Modern World"

Thanks

To the Dorothy Sargent Rosenberg Poetry Foundation for selecting "Inch" and "Visions at Birch Creek" as award recipients.

To Rick Lupert for making me *Poetry Super Highway*'s "Poet of the Week" on my birthday.

To Chandra Dickson and Abby Norwood for nominating "All This for a Dollar" and "Lima" for the Pushcart Prize.

To Tyler Chadwick for anthologizing "Inch," "Jerusalem Artichoke," and "Moose Remembered" in *Fire in the Pasture* (Peculiar Pages Press).

To Ted Badger at *Lucidity* for awarding the one-dollar prize to "Reading up on the Qur'an in a McDonald's Playland."

About the Author

Matthew James Babcock is Professor of English at BYU–Idaho in Rexburg. His debut chapbook, *Points of Reference*, is available from Folded Word. Winner of the 2016 Juxtaprose Poetry Prize, he also received a 2008 Dorothy Sargent Rosenberg Poetry Award, and has been thrice nominated for the Pushcart Prize. His creative nonfiction has been listed as "notable" in *Best American Essays*, and Press 53 selected his novella, *He Wanted to Be a Cartoonist for* The New Yorker, as a first-prize winner in its Open Awards Anthology. His academic work can be found in *The Journal of Ecocriticism* and *Private Fire: The Ecopoetry and Prose of Robert Francis*. His debut fiction collection, *Future Perfect*, is forthcoming from Ferry Street Books, and his debut essay collection, *Heterodoxologies*, will be released soon from Educe Press.

www.ingramcontent.com/pod-product-compliance
Lightning Source LLC
Chambersburg PA
CBHW021405090426
42742CB00009B/1022
9781941196366